Samuel Arthur Bent

The Wayside Inn

Its History and Literature

Samuel Arthur Bent

The Wayside Inn
Its History and Literature

ISBN/EAN: 9783337155025

Printed in Europe, USA, Canada, Australia, Japan

Cover: Foto ©ninafisch / pixelio.de

More available books at **www.hansebooks.com**

THE WAYSIDE INN

ITS HISTORY AND LITERATURE

AN ADDRESS

Delivered before the

SOCIETY OF
COLONIAL WARS

at the

WAYSIDE INN, SUDBURY, MASSACHUSETTS
JUNE 17, 1897

BY

SAMUEL ARTHUR BENT
Member of the Council

Boston
1897

THE WAYSIDE INN, ITS HISTORY AND LITERATURE.

Mr. Governor and Gentlemen:

This old town of Sudbury, to which on an anniversary dear to Massachusetts we make our summer pilgrimage, was one of the earliest inland settlements of the Bay Colony. The population on tide water was pressed by increasing immigration as early as 1637, and in that year it was proposed that a company should proceed westward from Watertown, "owing," as the record has it, "to straitness of accommodation and want of more meadow." Concord was already settled to the northward, and when in 1638 men of Watertown and Cambridge pushed their way into the wilderness, they formed the nineteenth township in the Colony, obtaining the grant of a tract of land five miles square, bounded east by Watertown, that part now Weston, north by Concord, south and west by the wilderness. Their route had been, however, already marked out for them. Through the south-east corner of their settlement passed the Indian trail, or the "old Connecticut path," along this very road from the sea-board to Connecticut, by which the ministers Hooker, Stone, their companions and families, had already journeyed towards the settlement of Hartford.

Our settlers were joined here by others coming direct from England, several of them, Haynes, Noyes, Bent,

Rutter, and Goodenow, fellow-passengers in the "good shipp 'Confidence'" sailing from Southampton, April 24, 1638, meeting on this common settling-ground Stone, of Cambridge, Parmenter, Treadway, Pelham, and Browne, of Watertown, and here, to the number of fifty-four, building their cabins looking into the darkness of the wilderness beyond.

It was natural that they should ask their pastor, the Rev. Edmund Browne, to name their settlement. He had come from England in 1637, and from his early home in Suffolkshire or from that of some of his family he called the town Sudbury, which was confirmed by the General Court in 1639 in the act of incorporation. And not only did he name it Sudbury, but he gave another Suffolk name to a section of it, Lanham, from the town spelled Lavenham, but pronounced Lanham on the other side of the water.

There exists no record of the dimensions of any of the first dwelling-houses of Sudbury, but we may judge something of their size by the specifications in a lease of a house to be built by Edmund Rice prior to the year 1655. It was certainly a very small house, "thirty foot long, ten foot high, one foot sill from the ground, sixteen foot wide, with two rooms, both below or one above the other, all the doors, walls, stairs with convenient fixtures and well planked under foot, and boarded sufficiently to lay corn in the story above head." Their earliest dwellings may have been even simpler, with the most scanty furniture, teaming being difficult from Watertown over the new road to Sudbury.

Sudbury had rich natural advantages for a successful settlement. The town was well watered; the heavy timber covering much of the land was free from underbrush; wild fowl, turkeys, pigeons, grouse, were plentiful; game was abundant, in the pursuit of which the Indians had made clearings; while broad meadows lined the river and brooks. The settlers were all young men, the emigrants from England were also in the prime of manhood, and for many years not an old man was to be seen in the settlement. They prospered within their own limits, and pushed still further, sending their sons into the wilderness to build up other settlements; to Worcester, Grafton, and Rutland, forming municipalities within their own borders or adjacent to them, as Framingham and Marlborough. But one cloud rested upon their horizon, threatening them as all frontier and outpost settlements, until the storm of Indian invasion burst upon them, and every habitation, save sheepcotes, was swept into destruction.

Among the early settlers was one John How, a glover by trade. He was admitted a freeman in 1641 and was chosen selectman the next year. In 1655 he was appointed "to see to the restraining of youth on the Lord's day." He was a petitioner for Marlborough plantation in 1657, moved there about the same year, and was elected a selectman. He was the first tavern keeper in that town, having a public house as early as 1661. "At this ordinary," says the historian of Sudbury, "his grandson, who afterwards kept the Sudbury Red Horse Tavern, may have been favorably struck with the occupation of an innholder and thus led to establish the business at Sudbury."

The proximity of John How's house in Marlborough to the Indian plantation brought him into direct contact with his savage neighbors, and by his kindness he gained their confidence and good will, and they accordingly not only respected his rights, but often made him their umpire in cases of difficulty. He acquired, I have read, the reputation of a Solomon by his decision of a dispute where a pumpkin vine sprang up within the premises of one Indian and the fruit ripened upon the land of another. The question of the ownership of the pumpkin was referred to him, when he called for a knife and divided the fruit, giving half to each claimant. This struck the parties as the perfection of justice, and fixed the impartiality of the judge on an immutable basis. John How died in 1680, at the age of seventy-eight years, and left an estate valued at £511.

His son Samuel, a carpenter by trade, born in 1642, married, in 1663, Martha Bent, daughter of John Bent, of Sudbury, the first of that name; and later widow Clapp, of Hingham. He is described as a man of great energy and public spirit. He could at any rate have given points to any real estate dealer of the present day on the expansive power of the English language as applied to land, as will be seen from the following incident. He entered into a land speculation with one Gookin, of Cambridge, sheriff of Middlesex County, a son of Major Gookin, well known as a writer, soldier, and friend of the Christian Indians. They bought, in 1682, of the Natick Indians a tract said in the deed to contain " by estimation two hundred acres more or less." The western boundary was not specified in the deed, and the words " more or less," when applied to " waste land," so called, were understood to give the purchaser a wide latitude. How and Gookin accordingly took possession of all the unoccupied land between Cochituate pond on the east and Sudbury river on the west, parcelled it out, and sold lots from time to time to *bona fide* purchasers. The Indians at length became dissatisfied and complained to the General Court of encroachments upon the grant of 1682. How and Gookin submitted to a committee of the court their deed, and a writing from some of the Indians for an enlargement of the grant, and a receipt for money paid in consideration thereof. The committee found that under these writings How and Gookin had sold *1,700* acres north of the Worcester turnpike, which was confirmed by the General Court, and *1,000* acres south of the turnpike, which was not allowed, but remained in possession of the Indians, and later became a factor in a land controversy between the towns of Sherborn and Framingham.

In 1702 Samuel How gave his son David, born in 1674, a tract of one hundred and thirty acres of the so-called " new grant " of Sudbury, and on one of the lots of this grant, bounded easterly on the highway and westerly by Marlborough, David How began immediately to build a house. During its erection tradition says that the work-men resorted at night for protection against Indian attacks to the Parmenter garrison house, half a mile away. Soon after its construction How opened it as a public house, the fifth tavern on the road from Boston westwards. In a letter to an English lady, dated Dec. 28, 1863, Longfellow gives his version of the genesis of this house. "Some two hundred years ago," he says, " an English family by the name of Howe built there (in Sudbury) a country house, which has remained in the family down to the present time, the last of the race dying about two years ago. Losing their fortune, they became innkeepers, and for a century the Red Horse has flourished, going down from father to son. The place is just as I have described it, though no longer an inn. All this will account for the landlord's coat of arms, and his being a justice of the peace, and his being known as the squire, things that must sound strange in English ears." That a man of good family should open a public house in the early days of our New England towns would not to those who have read the history of the times need either explanation or apology. The institution of taverns in these towns followed quickly upon their settlement. Being a recognized need in a new and thinly settled country, no one thought of speaking of them as an evil, or even as a necessary evil. That travellers and sojourners might be provided for, taverns were licensed by the General Court as fast as new villages sprang up. Supervision was strict, as the spirit of a patriarchal community founded on morals would require. An innkeeper was not then looked upon as a person who was pursuing a disgraceful or immoral calling. He was generally a responsible and respectable member of the village community. His house, closely watched by the constable, whose business it was to know everybody else's business, became a landmark for the community. Streets in towns like Boston were named from the taverns situated on them, and in the country the signs which bore the rude effigy of a horse or a bull, a star or a sun, were hailed by the weary traveller as offering " all the comforts of home."

Nor do I find that David How was compelled by a reverse of fortune to open his house to the public. He was one of a family of thirteen children of Samuel How. One of the local historians says that these thirteen made an assignment in 1714, the year in which, according to some authorities, the house was opened. No such assignment is on record in Middlesex County, so far as I can discover. The administrator of Samuel How's estate certified to the injury it would receive if divided among so many heirs, and administration was accordingly continued for several years. I am told by Mr. Homer Rogers, who bought this estate after the death of the last Howe, that in examining the title for the first deed of the property for nearly two hundred years no record of any assignment, attachment, or other incumbrance was found upon it.

It may be supposed that David How, one of so large a family, found it necessary to earn his living by a respectable calling, and the business of his grandfather in Marlborough would naturally suggest that of an innkeeper.

He accordingly opened his house to the public, not the first man in Sudbury to do so, but destined to eclipse them all in the celebrity of his inn and the fame of his descendants. His house, then called simply "How's Tavern in Sudbury" to distinguish it from How's Tavern in Marlborough, soon became known. Thus in 1716 Judge Sewall records in his diary that he started with a friend for Springfield on the 27th of April. He says he "treated at N. Sparhawk's, got to How's in Sudbury about one-half hour by the sun." The original house was a small one, generally supposed, says Mr. Rogers, to be the L in the rear of the present edifice, although others speak of some part of it as standing as late as 1829, implying that the original structure has by this time disappeared.

David How kept the tavern until his death in 1746, when it passed into the hands of his son Ezekiel, by whom it was enlarged as increased business made necessary. Receiving the custom of the great highway and mail route from Boston westward, the old inn of one story was merged in a more elaborate structure of two stories with a gambrel roof and arms spreading on either side, receiving through its seventy-nine windows alike the summer's and the winter's sun.[1]

Its new proprietor christened his inn the "Red Horse Tavern," to distinguish it from the "Black Horse" of Marlborough, and hung in front of it a sign, one side of which bore the effigy of a fiery steed, while on the other were later seen the initials of the first three owners:

D. H.	.	.	.	.	1686
E. H.	.	.	.	.	1746
A. Howe	.	.	.	.	1796

---

[1] The photograph, of which the frontispiece is a reproduction, was taken June 17, 1897, by Mr. Arthur Cecil Thomson, of the Society of Colonial Wars.

For years this sign swung to the breeze and bore the heat of summer and the blasts of winter, and was un-doubtedly showing its weather-beaten and half-obliterated features when Longfellow saw it on the visit which was to immortalize the Red Horse Tavern as the " Wayside Inn," for he included it in the picture of the house:

> " Half effaced by rain and shine
> The Red Horse prances on the sign."

But the old sign has disappeared just as the old name gave way to the newer title.

It was during the incumbency, if I may use the word, of Ezekiel How that a price list was established at Sud-bury for various commodities, and the following tariff for taverns would not tempt our new proprietor of 1897 to embark in a business which promised so little profit on the financial basis of the last century.   It reads thus:

Mug best India flip	15
New England do	12
Toddy in proportion	
A good dinner	20
Common do	12
Best supper and breakfast	15 each
Common do	12
Lodging	4

I cannot as one " to the manner born " describe this house, with its many rooms given to public use and its apartments private to the landlord's family.

Entering the house and turning to the right, we find the tap-room, in the most ancient-looking part of the house. In one corner over the bar is the wooden portcullis, which rose to the call for refreshments, or fell as trade was dull.

We still see the ancient floor, worn more deeply than in any other room, overhead the heavy timbers, the very oak of which is seasoned with the spicy vapor of the steaming flagons. Upstairs you are shown the travellers' rooms which those of lesser note occupied in common, and the state chamber still decorated with its wall paper of blue-bells, where tradition says Lafayette slept on his journey to Boston, in 1824. Above in the garret the slaves were accommodated, and when Indian invasion was feared grain was stored there against a siege. In one of the upper rooms was the dance hall, which was later placed in an annex to the ancient building. In the more modern room the dais still stands at one end for the players, the wooden benches are still fixed to the walls, the floor is smoothly polished by feet once swiftly tripping in the old-fashioned contra dances or the stately minuet. Gone are the dancers, silent is the violin, over all the place for thirty years has reigned a solemn stillness save when it is broken by the sweet voices of Nature and Nature's offspring, or, as Parsons sang of it:

"The 'scutcheon is faded that hangs on the wall,
 And the hearth looks forlorn in the desolate hall;
 And the floor that has bent with the minuet's tread
 Is like a church pavement — the dancers are dead."

Could we have passed a day under the hospitable roof of the Red Horse Tavern one hundred and fifty years ago, those four and twenty hours would have enrolled before us a perfect picture of New England life. Long before daylight our sleep would have been disturbed by the rumbling of the heavy market wagons, taking to Boston produce of the garden and the farm from western Massachusetts, even from New York, and from intermediate places along the route. Later in the day we should see

them filling with heavy wheels and large canvastops the
spacious lawn in front of the house, returning empty from
their destination, their drivers refreshing themselves in the
tap-room while their horses were baited in the barns.   On
our descent for breakfast the music of a horn winding
through the valley announced the arrival of the mail-
coach from Boston, which started on its journey at three
o'clock in the morning, its inmates silent like so many
shadows, until the rising sun clothed them with forms and
touched them like Memnon's statue with speech.   The
black stable-boys rushed to take out the horses, the maids
stood attendant behind the tables hot with the morning
fare, mine host himself, erect in military dignity, stood at
the door as the travellers emerged from their pent-up
quarters, cramped and dusty and eager to break their fast
after a journey of three and twenty good English miles
from the Town House in Boston.   Before the tavern was
opened this road was a mail route; in fact, from 1704,
when appeared the first newspaper in America, a western
post was carried with greater or less regularity, and travellers availed themselves of the post rider's company over
a tedious and sometimes dangerous road.   It was in such
company that Madame Knight made her famous journey
on horseback from Boston to New York in the very year
we have mentioned, 1704, and in the curious account of
it which she wrote, she says that at Mr. Haven's[1] she
could get no sleep because of the clamor of some of the
" town topers " in the next room, discussing over their
cups the signification of the Indian word "Narragansett."
So she says that she finally fell to her old way of compos-
ing her resentment as follows:

" I ask thy aid, O potent Rum,
    To charm these wrangling topers dum.

---

[1] A tavern in what is now North Kingston, R.I.

> Thou hast their giddy brains possest —
> The man confounded with the beast —
> And I, poor I, can get no rest.
> Intoxicate them with thy fumes,
> O still their tongues till morning comes!"

"And I know not," she adds, "but my wishes took effect; for the dispute soon ended with t'other dram; and so good-night!"

Returning now to our inn, when the mail-coach had pursued its journey with a refreshed and consequently better-natured company, a travelling chariot with four well-groomed bays, coachman and footman in livery, with trim lady's maid and prim duenna, caused even a greater sensation than the more plebeian mail-coach with its heterogeneous company. A dainty lady, dressed in the fashion of the day, alighted for an hour's refreshment, amid the open-mouthed wonder of the onlookers, just as some years later Dorothy Quincy paused on her journey to Bridgeport to meet John Hancock, whom she married at Mr. Burr's, in that distant town. And before she started on her way again she exchanged greetings with a solemn deputy travelling on horseback from Springfield to the General Court, arrayed, like travellers of that time, with riding coat and "stirrup-stockings," and well-filled saddle-bags. So important a personage Colonel How greeted with cordial but respectful familiarity, and invited to partake of cheer a little more choice than the ordinary traveller could expect even at the famous sign of the Red Horse.

But while the travelling statesman was giving our host his views on public affairs a novel sound struck the ear. A distant drum brought the boys and the maids and the tap-room loafers to doors and windows. Soon the shrill music of the wry-necked fife lent the melody of the

"Road to Boston" to the rataplan of the drum. Bay-onets gleamed in the sunlight striking through the heavy foliage of the oaks, and a dusty company of foot soldiers tramped along the road. "Halt!" cried the captain, opposite the door. Arms were stacked, ranks were broken, the landlord showed the officers into the room behind the bar, while the men stretched them-selves upon the grass under the oaks, which were old then, and well grown when, nearly a century earlier, Wadsworth and Brocklebank marched under them to their glorious death.

All through our New England history the Red Horse was a favorite resting-place of the New England soldiery, mindful of its proverbial good cheer. As long ago as 1724, during Lovewell's war, this tap-room was the ren-dezvous of the troop of horse, steel-capped and buff-coated, that patrolled the roads hereabout. Later, the troops hurrying to the frontier in the French and Indian wars, to Ticonderoga and Crown Point, shook the dust from what it would be sarcasm to call their "uniforms," before this house. Later still, the Worcester minute-men, led by Timothy Bigelow, rested here on their forced march at the Lexington alarm, until the distant rumbling of Percy's cannon hurried them to the front, and from still further away Putnam and Arnold and the Connecticut militia may have asked their way at this house, whose landlord himself had buckled on his sword and ridden to the fray with the men of Sudbury.

Ezekiel How, at the outbreak of hostilities in 1775, was lieutenant-colonel of the Fourth Regiment of Middle-sex County Militia, of which James Barrett, of Concord, was colonel. The next year, May 10, he was chosen by the Legislature as colonel of the regiment, and held his commission until Jan. 26, 1779, when he resigned.

At the time of the Lexington alarm, one-fifth of the

entire population of Sudbury was enrolled in the six
companies of the town, and the number in actual service
at Concord and Lexington was three hundred and two.
Word came between three and four o'clock on the morning
of the 19th of April to the Sudbury member of the Pro-
vincial Congress, by an express from Concord, that the
British were on their way to that town. The church bell
was rung, musketry was discharged, and by sunrise the
greater part of the population was notified. The men of
this town had already received "the baptism of fire."
They had learned of war since it had been brought to
their very doors by the savage warriors of King Philip,
and in the intervening period one hundred names of
Sudbury's sons are found on the muster rolls of the suc-
cessive French and Indian wars.

"The morning of the 19th was unusually fine," wrote
later a Revolutionary soldier, "and the inhabitants of
Sudbury never can make such an important appearance
probably again. Every countenance seemed to discover
the importance of the event." The Sudbury companies
took two different routes to Concord, and on their arrival
two of them, commanded by Captains Nixon and
Haynes, with Lieutenant-Colonel How, who accompa-
nied them, started for the old North Bridge. "When
they came within sight of Colonel Barrett's house they
halted," says the historian of Sudbury; "before them
were the British, engaged in their mischievous work.
Gun carriages had been collected and piled together to
be burned, the torch already had been applied, and the
residence of the colonel had been ransacked. They
halted, and Colonel How exclaimed, 'If any blood has
been shed, not one of the rascals shall escape!' Dis-
guising himself, he rode on to ascertain the truth." It
was probably not far from nine o'clock when this event
took place, which shows the celerity with which the Sud-

bury troops had moved. Shattuck, in his history, says
that two companies from Sudbury, under How, Nixon,
and Haynes, came to Concord, and having received or-
ders from a person stationed at the entrance to the town
to proceed to the North instead of to the South Bridge,
arrived at Colonel Barrett's just before the British soldiers retreated, which is confirmed by the statement of
the Revolutionary soldier before quoted, that "the Sudbury companies were but a short distance from the
North Bridge when the first opposition was made to the
haughty enemy." At any rate the Sudbury companies
joined in the pursuit of the retreating British, and in at
least two of the sharp encounters which occurred, one
at Merriam's Corner and the other at Hardy's Hill, they
bravely bore their part. They sustained a loss of two
men killed and one wounded, and it is an interesting
fact, mentioned last year in the dedication of the Revolutionary Soldiers' Monument, that Sudbury possessed
at this time "a class of men who were exempt from military service because of non-age or old age, or some
other disability, and that those persons would not be
kept at home, but went to Concord and Lexington on
horseback." One of these had a bullet put through his
coat, the horse of another was shot under him, and Dea-
con Josiah Haynes, who at the age of seventy-nine years
had pursued the British towards Lexington, was killed.

I may be pardoned if, speaking on my ancestral
although not on my native heath, I mention another
man, of my own name, the aged Thomas Bent, who went
to Lexington on horseback, and received a bullet-wound
in one of his legs, from the effect of which he soon after-
ward died. Mr. Bent, after being wounded, started for
his home in East Sudbury, and while on the road met his
son, a lad in his teens, who, like his three brothers, was
hurrying to the fray. Instead of asking the boy to

return with his wounded father, he urged him to the front, and the boy obeyed and went.

I do not find that Colonel How took further part in the active operations of the Revolution. He continued to command his militia regiment, members of which were drawn for service in the Continental Army, many of them in the regiment commanded by that valiant soldier of Framingham and Sudbury, who had won his spurs at Louisburg, Colonel, afterwards General, John Nixon, and the muster-rolls describe these soldiers as " of the fourth regiment of foot, commanded by Col. Ezekiel How." On the other hand, the town records show that the colonel, now one of her important citizens, served on committees to make up quotas, prepare the muster rolls, and " estimate the services of each particular person in Sudbury in the present war." These lists prove the patriotic spirit of the town, which had not a Tory within her borders, but which with a population of 2,160, being the largest town in Middlesex County, with about 500 ratable polls, sent to different service during the war from 400 to 500 men, 100 men in three companies on the glorious day which we are now celebrating, others later with Washington in New York, against Burgoyne in the North, and farther on braving the rigors of a Canadian winter, in the attempt to gain Canada to the Continental cause. Well might Washington honor this town and this inn with a brief visit, stopping here to lunch on his triumphal but peaceful progress through New England in 1789, shaking hands with one of the heroes of Concord fight, and recalling to the survivors of the Revolution their unshaken fidelity to the cause now so gloriously victorious. We know what he must have said; we echo the words which thrilled the men and women who thronged about the " Father of his Country," " Honor, eternal honor, to the patriots of Sudbury ! "

Colonel How died in 1796. In the inventory of his
estate we find the famous coat of arms appraised at $4,
his firearms at $8, his library at $10, the clock at $30,
a silver tankard at $25, and other plate at $30, the home-
stead with 240 acres of land at $6,500, the entire appraisal
amounting to $9,531.48. We see by his will that the
inn then consisted of new and old parts, for it speaks of
" a new kitchen at the west end of the dwelling-house,
with the lower room adjoining thereto, also the long
chamber over the aforesaid room, with the north-west
bed-chamber in the old part of said dwelling-house."
He left most of the personal articles before mentioned to
his " well-beloved granddaughter, Hepsibah Brown,"
and, after many minor legacies, the residue of his estate
to his third son, Adam How.

This third proprietor of the Red Horse Tavern was
the antiquarian of the family. The ancient coat-of-arms,
hanging during his boyhood in the parlor of the inn,
gave his thoughts an heraldic turn, and he was proud of
the lineage he derived from an English ancestry. Longfellow could have said of him, as of his son, —

> " Proud was he of his name and race,
> Of old Sir William, and Sir Hugh,
> And in the parlor, full in view,
> His coat-of-arms, well-framed and glazed,
> Upon the wall in colors blazed;
> He beareth gules upon his shield,
> A chevron argent in the field,
> With three wolf's heads, and for the crest
> A Wyvern part-per-pale addressed
> Upon a helmet barred; below
> The scroll reads, ' By the name of Howe.' "

It was Adam How who put into circulation the How
genealogy, founded on a tradition which traced the

family from John How of Sudbury, son of John How of Watertown, to a Warwickshire ancestor, son of John How of Hodinhull, connected with "the most noble and puissant Lord Charles How," created Baron How of Wormton by James I., and Earl of Lancaster by Charles I., and descended from Hugh, a favorite of Edward II., all of which was inscribed among the scrolls and leaves and other devices of the coat-of-arms, surmounted by a "Wyvern," a two-legged, winged creature, with the head of a dragon, an heraldic cockatrice as fabulous as the genealogy over which it hissed its vipery head. One of the learned historians of Framingham dismisses the genealogy by saying he has failed to discover its confirmation in the records of Watertown, and Savage condemned the attempt to connect this family with a title extinct nearly two hundred years before the emigration.[1] But we shall not complain if the pale light of tradition continues to play around this coat-of-arms as around so many in our New England mansions, equally elaborate and imaginary.

Adam How kept the inn until 1830 and was succeeded by his son Lyman, who was born in 1801, and was found dead in his bed in 1861. It is with him and with his times that we are brought into more intimate acquaintance by the genius of Longfellow, who gathered in his "Prelude" to the "Tales" the traditions of the house and of its proprietors. We read of this last hero of the family that Squire Howe, as the name had come to be spelled, was a man rather imposing in appearance, somewhat dignified and grave. He was at one time leader of the choir of the Congregational church, which was assisted in its musical efforts before the introduction of organs by a violin, bass viol, and clarionet. He was a member of the school committee and a justice of the peace, and for

years was a familiar figure to the villagers of South Sudbury, riding in his chaise with the top tipped back, as he
went to the post-office or to visit the district schools.   In
his younger and more prosperous days he is said to have
fitly represented the family of Howe, of which, dying
unmarried, he closed this line.

On the occasion of the gathering of the Howe family
in 1871, one of its members wrote : " As a house of enter-
tainment the inn was always characterized by its good
order and hospitality, and not less by the sumptuous
table with which it refreshed the hungry traveller.   Before the innovation of railroads several stages made their
daily call at this house, stopping long enough to change
horses and allow the passengers, often from remote sec-
tions of the country, sometimes from foreign lands, to
breakfast and dine."   The mention of the introduction
of railroads brings us to the close of the long career of
this house as a public resort.   As his years increased and
as travellers were whirled by steam past hill and dale,
landlord Howe's business became smaller and smaller,
until his sudden death closed the record of the inn.   His
dirge was sung by a faithful frequenter, Dr. Parsons :

> "Thunder clouds may roll above him,
>   And the bolt may rend his oak ;
>   Lyman lieth where no longer
>   He shall dread the lightning stroke.

> "Never to his father's hostel
>   Comes a kinsman or a guest ;
>   Midnight calls for no more candles ;
>   House and landlord both have rest.

" Fetch my steed !   I cannot linger.
Buckley, quick !   I must away.
Good old groom, take thou this nothing;
Millions could not make me stay."

After Mr. Howe's death the place was sold with its
contents. Fabulous tales were told of the rare antique
furniture and other articles, and of the fancy prices they
brought, but the inventory showed nothing more valuable
than Lyman's sister's spinet, the first instrument of its kind
brought into this town, on whose ivory keys the moon-
light played " inaudible melodies " in Longfellow's " Prelude," and which was valued at $25. For many years
this antique piano was in Sudbury village, but to-day is
again to be seen in the parlor of this inn, where Miss
Jerusha used to play on it the " Battle of Prague," and
to whose accompaniment she would sing, " in a thin and
decorous voice," the strains of " Highland Mary," once so
fashionable.   Some of the heirlooms of the house became
the property of Mr. Howe's distant relative, Miss Eaton,
including " fair Princess Mary's pictured face," a half
length mezzotint engraving of a daughter of George II.
Here came to an honorable repose

" The sword the landlord's grandsire bore
In the rebellious days of yore,"

the scabbard immovably rusted within its sheath, its hilt
mounted with ivory and silver.   And to her came the
silver spurs worn by Colonel How at Concord fight, and
his silver buckles for stock, knees, and shoes.   But gone
are many furnishings which have figured in descriptions
of the "Wayside Inn," like the little desk in the tap-
room, where the tipplers' score was set down, like the
pewter flagons before whose spicy vapors sat grave depu-

ties, with perchance a parson or a magistrate.   Gone from
the window-sash, but still preserved for us to-day, is that
invitation, homely but redolent of good cheer, almost the
only thing save the bare walls which takes us to the good
old days of the Red Horse Tavern, scratched on a window-
pane June 24, 1774, by "William Molineaux, Jr., Esq.,"
son of a patriot friend of Adams and Otis:

> "What do you think,
>   Here is good drink,
>   Perhaps you may not know it,
>   If not in haste do stop and taste,
>   You merry folks will show it."

The poet of the Wayside Inn did not attempt to
dignify this rhyme by transferring it to the "Prelude" to
his "Tales," after asking Miss Eaton to copy it for him,
but he included a reference to it in his description of the
house, as

> "Flashing on the window-pane,
>   Emblazoned with its light and shade,
>   The jovial rhymes that still remain,
>   Writ near a century ago,
>   By the great Major Molineaux,
>   Whom Hawthorne has immortal made."

Longfellow here chose to connect by way of compli-
ment the hero of Hawthorne's imaginary tar-and-feathery
story with the author of this jingle, and the great novelist
thanked the great poet for the line in a letter written
from Concord, Jan. 12, 1864: "It gratifies my mind to
find my own name shining in your verse, — even as if I
had been gazing up at the moon, and detected my own
features in its profile."

I confess that there is something pathetic in the
extinction of an honorable race, even of innkeepers,
whose gradual decline touches us like the ruin of a royal
family, " fallen from their high estate," and forced to eat
the bread of exile. But now behold the resurrection —
not of this family, but of this house, under the wand of
the magician, and tell me if even the poet's art has ever
wrought a metamorphosis more sudden or more complete
than this.

It is possible that Longfellow stopped, when a young
man, at the Red Horse Tavern on his way to New York
to sail for Europe; but the only visit we know him to
have made was after Lyman Howe's death. Writing in
his journal Oct. 31, 1862, he says :

"Drive with Fields to the old Red Horse Tavern in
Sudbury — alas! no longer an inn! A lovely valley,
the winding road shaded by grand old oaks before the
house. A rambling, tumble-down old building, two
hundred years old." And when he came to sing of it in
verse his prose is thus transformed —

> " A region of repose it seems,
> A place of slumber and of dreams,
> Remote among the wooded hills ! "

And of the house —

> "Built in the old Colonial Day
> When men lived in a grander way,
> With ampler hospitality;
> A kind of old Hobgoblin Hall,
> Now somewhat fallen to decay,
> With weather-stains upon the wall,
> And chimneys huge, and tiled, and tall."

He immediately resolved to make this old house, henceforth rechristened as "the Wayside Inn," the scene of the meeting of friends who, like the pilgrims of Chaucer, were to tell their tales "one autumn night" when

> "Across the meadows bare and brown
> The windows in the way side inn
> Gleamed red with firelight through the leaves
> Of woodbine, hanging from the eaves
> Their crimson curtains rent and thin."

In his journal of November 11 he speaks of having completed five of the "Tales" supposed to have been told here; on the 18th he finished the "Prelude," and early in the following spring his "Sudbury Tales," as he first called them, were in press. Published in the following November as "Tales of a Wayside Inn," fifteen thousand copies were at once sold, and they took their place with the most popular of the poet's compositions, and soon *a* Wayside Inn became *the* Wayside Inn forevermore. Longfellow admitted to an interviewer that he drew his idea not only from Chaucer, but from the Decameron of Boccaccio, and that the inn served as a framework for the tales. "They are drawn," says his biographer, "from various sources. To Mr. Longfellow belongs the charm of their telling, often with much amplification and adornment. In perhaps only one instance, 'The Birds of Killingworth,' is the story of his own invention."

In the "Prelude" Longfellow introduces his friends, who are to tell their stories

> "before the firelight shedding over all
> The splendor of its ruddy glow,
> Filling the parlor large and low,"

after the landlord has opened with that best known of them all, "Paul Revere's Ride." He first introduces us to "a student of old books and days," Henry Ware Wales. This, one of the least known of all the "*dramatis personæ*," graduated at Harvard College in 1838 in the same class with James Russell Lowell, William W. Story, Dr. George B. Loring, and among the very few still living, Mr. William I. Bowditch and Dr. Samuel L. Abbot. He studied medicine, but never practised; was brought to Longfellow's attention by his great love of rare volumes, lived much abroad, and died in Paris in 1856 after a surgical operation. One of his brothers was the late George W. Wales, a munificent patron of art in Boston. Then there was the

"young Sicilian
In sight of Ætna born and bred,"

Professor Luigi Monti, the only survivor of this immortal band.

" A Spanish Jew from Alicant
With aspect grand and grave was there,"

Israel Edrehi,

"Vendor of silks and fabrics rare.
Well versed was he in Hebrew books,
Talmud and Targum and the lore
Of Kabala,"

and from him Longfellow derived much of the rabbinical learning which he introduced into the "Golden Legend."

The "theologian from the school of Cambridge on the Charles" was Professor Treadwell, of the Divinity School, who passed many summers at the inn, as did the "poet," Dr. Parsons,

> " Who did not find his sleep less sweet
>   For music in some neighboring street."

In his poem on " Guy Fawkes's Day in Sudbury Inn "
Parsons brings Longfellow into the company there, even
as Longfellow had already brought them together in his
greater poem, and with that freedom from jealousy just
alluded to, Parsons

>   " to sweeten the toast
> Gave the noblest of poets Massachusetts can boast!
> Famous now is the house in whose halls he hath been,
> For his muse hath made sacred old Sudbury Inn! "

Lastly there was the musician,

> " Every feature of his face
>   Revealing his Norwegian race,"

Ole Bull, " the angel of the violin; " and when its music
ceased,

>   " began
> A clamor for the landlord's tale,"

who then opens the series

> " In idle moments, idly told,"

until all the tales are finished, when

> " Farewell! the portly landlord cried;
>   Farewell! the parting guests replied,
>   But little thought that nevermore
>   Their feet would pass that threshold o'er."

And now *my* " Tale of a Wayside Inn " is told, the story of the lives and fortunes of Adam and Lyman, of David and Ezekiel. We have seen how the oldest and most famous inn of the country, the " Red Horse Tavern," disappeared, and on its site arose the " Wayside Inn," now moss-grown with tradition, and bathed in the after-glow of a poet's imagination. Hither began to wend their way pilgrims from this land and from all lands, until their number was swollen to thousands in these later years, many of whom had never heard of the " Red Horse Tavern," but to all of whom the " Wayside Inn " had become a household word. And one wiser and more prescient than the rest wrote: " The time will surely come when the sign of the Red Horse will swing before the Wayside Inn again, and pilgrims from far and near, from Boston and Sicily and Alicant, students, musicians, theologians, poets, shall gather in the autumn evenings around the blazing fires, enjoyers of a finer hospitality than any known of yore."

And lo! the prophet's words fall true, and again the doors of the " Wayside Inn " fly open to the expected guests; the descendants of the men of earlier days recall around these tables the " good old colony times;" and perchance a twentieth century gallant may write on a newer pane:

> " What do *you* think,
> Here is good drink,
> Perhaps you may not know it."

Mr. Governor and fellow-members, let me be your toast-master to-day. Representing indirectly four generations of worthy hosts, let me wish " renewed prosperity, long, aye, a still longer life, to the Red Horse Tavern of ancient Sudbury ! "